Get CONNECTED to DIGITAL LITERACY

COMPUTING and CODING in the REAL WORLD

Clive Gifford

Crabtree Publishing Company

www.crabtreebooks.com

Crabtree Publishing Company
www.crabtreebooks.com
1-800-387-7650

Published in Canada
Crabtree Publishing
616 Welland Ave.
St. Catharines, ON
L2M 5V6

Published in the United States
Crabtree Publishing
PMB 59051, 350 Fifth Ave.
59th Floor,
New York, NY

Published in 2018 by CRABTREE PUBLISHING COMPANY.

First published in 2017 by Wayland
(A division of Hachette Children's Books)
Copyright © Hodder & Stoughton 2017

Author: Clive Gifford
Project editor: Sonya Newland
Designer: Tim Mayer
Editors: Sonya Newland, Kathy Middleton
Proofreader: Petrice Custance
Prepress technician: Ken Wright
Print and production coordinator: Margaret Amy Salter

Consultant: Lee Martin, B. Ed, E-Learning Specialist

Photographs:
All images courtesy of Shutterstock except iStock: p. 20b (ttsz).

While every attempt has been made to clear copyright, should there be any inadvertent omission this will be rectified in future editions.

Disclaimer: The website addresses (URLs) included in this book were valid at the time of going to press. However, because of the nature of the Internet, it is possible that some addresses may have changed, or sites may have changed or closed down since publication. While the author and publisher regret any inconvenience this may cause the readers, no responsibility for any such changes can be accepted by either the author or the publisher.

Note to reader: Words highlighted in bold appear in the Glossary on page 30.
Answers to activities are on page 31.

Printed in the USA/072017/CG20170524

Library and Archives Canada Cataloguing in Publication

Gifford, Clive, author
    Computing and coding in the real world / Clive Gifford.

(Get connected to digital literacy)
Includes index.
Issued in print and electronic formats.
ISBN 978-0-7787-3621-9 (hardcover).--
ISBN 978-0-7787-3632-5 (softcover).--
ISBN 978-1-4271-1957-5 (HTML)

    1. Computer programming--Social aspects--Juvenile literature. 2. Computers--Social aspects--Juvenile literature. 3. Technology--Social aspects--Juvenile literature. I. Title.

QA76.6.G535 2017   j005.1   C2017-903179-1
                                          C2017-903180-5

Library of Congress Cataloging-in-Publication Data

CIP available at the Library of Congress

Contents

Computing All Around Us

Computers were once used only in huge science and military labs. Today, computing, which means work done by computers, is a part of so many things in our daily lives.

Inside guide

Inside your home, dozens of devices and household appliances feature computer technology. They run the microwave oven and fridge in your kitchen, and the **Bluetooth** speaker and **smart** TV in your living room. All smartphones, tablets, game consoles, and many other digital devices rely on computer technology. Much of the music and many of the TV shows you enjoy have also been created using computers.

The Internet

The Internet is a medium, or a place for communication, that links groups of computer **networks**. Hundreds of millions of computers around the world and other digital devices such as tablets and smartphones communicate with each other through the Internet. Whenever you send an email, use social media to share a photo or message, or surf websites on the **World Wide Web**, you are using the Internet.

Out in the open

Computing is everywhere outside the home, too, from barcode scanners to store checkouts to digital signs, and cash-dispensing bank machines. Computers manage traffic lights and other signals to keep vehicles moving smoothly, and in-car computers help guide cars to their destinations.

TRUE STORY

Poor Predictions! In 1943, the president of the computer company IBM, Thomas Watson, said: "I think there is a world market for maybe five computers." In 1977, Ken Olsen, who founded the computer company DEC, said: "There is no reason for any individual to have a computer in his home." Today, there are over two billion personal computers worldwide, and twice as many smartphones!

UP IN THE AIR

More than 70,000 aircraft fly through the skies above the United States every day. Each plane needs to be guided through its journey at the correct altitude, or height, to avoid colliding with other aircraft. Planes are guided by computer controls inside the aircraft as well as by human air traffic controllers in the airport's control tower.

Customers and computing

Many of the items you buy are designed on a computer, and then manufactured using computer-controlled machines. Some items are built by robots, which are controlled by computers. Computers are even involved in testing products as well as delivering products sold.

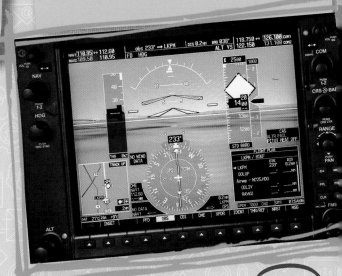

Input and Output

Computers need a way to interact with the real world. They have to be able to receive information and **output** the results in a way that can be used by people.

Processing and programs

The work is usually performed by the computer's **central processing unit (CPU)**. This is a microprocessor, often referred to as a chip. It can perform thousands or even millions of operations every second. The CPU runs a set of instructions called a program stored in the chip. The instructions are made up of lines of **code**. These are commands, or instructions, to the computer.

INPUT ····▶ PROCESSING ····▶ OUTPUT

STORAGE

FEEDBACK

Information flow

When **data** is put into a computer, it is called **input**. The computer works on the data in the next stage, called processing. The results may be stored and can be displayed now or later in a useful form called output. Sometimes, the output becomes new data for input. This information is called **feedback**.

TRUE STORY

Lightning Lines of Code. Some machines need vast amounts of code to run. The F-35 Lightning II aircraft features more than eight million lines of code in its programs to fly and navigate this military jet.

⬇ Input devices

A home or office computer uses input devices such as keyboards, a mouse, document scanners, and webcams. Common input devices on a smartphone or a tablet include touchscreens, microphones, and cameras. These devices gather information and send it for processing. Devices called **sensors** (see pages 12–13) also provide input in some computer systems.

Output from this iPad tablet are signals sent to the educational robot's motors, instructing them to move the robot's parts.

⬇ Output devices

Common output devices include speakers for sound, and monitor screens, which can display text, photos, and graphics. A printer provides people with a physical copy of the information worked on by the computer. Sometimes, a computer's output sends a series of signals to control electric motors or pumps to move parts of other machines.

A Virtual Reality headset game surrounds the player with a realistic, three-dimensional, or 3-D, view. The game's graphics and action are projected onto screens inside the headset.

pascal c# perl ruby python javascript java c++ ftp SQL visual basic PHP html ajax swift

Computer Languages

Computers don't read code written in English. They read code written in computer language, and there are hundreds of computer languages! Some languages, such as Scratch, Kodu, and Tynker, are for beginners just learning to program, or create code. Others, such as C, Python, and C++, are powerful languages that can be used to control major systems and machinery, from traffic light systems to **automated** factories.

7

All About Algorithms

Computer programs that control devices contain **algorithms**. These are a series of steps taken or rules followed to solve a problem or perform a certain task. Coders work hard to create accurate algorithms before they ever start writing program code.

Accurate algorithms

In coding, an algorithm must have all its steps explained extremely clearly and accurately. It's no good to simply tell a computer to "get dressed." The instructions to get dressed have to be broken down into many precise steps. The steps must also be in the right order. An algorithm that tells you to put on your shoes before you put on your socks simply wouldn't work!

Algorithms coded into digital cameras and smartphone camera **apps** help even inexperienced photographers take sharp, well-lit photographs.

STRETCH YOURSELF

Command a Robot

Try linking a series of simple steps together to make a robot perform different tasks at the following web address:

👉 http://lightbot.com/flash.html

Algorithms are used in navigation devices like this one, to find the shortest or quickest route to a destination.

YOU, THE COMPUTER

Algorithms are easier to understand when you realize that you use them every day. Without thinking about it, you perform a long series of steps each morning when you get out of bed. Before you head off to school, you have showered and brushed your teeth, dressed, and packed your backpack.

TRUE STORY

Costly Error! Mistakes in algorithms and programming can lead to big problems. When a new terminal at London's Heathrow Airport opened in 2008, errors in its baggage-handling computer programs led to more than 500 flights being canceled and thousands of bags not reaching their destination.

STRETCH YOURSELF

Toast Algorithm

Can you come up with all the steps to make a piece of buttered toast with jam? Think of all the steps required, however small, and list them in order.

☞ Have you included getting the jam out of the cupboard?

☞ Did you push the toaster button down?

☞ Did you get out a knife before your algorithm said to butter the toast?

Real-World Algorithms

Algorithms are at work all around you. They are in the music files you listen to on your tablet or music player, as well as in the controls of smart central-heating systems found in many homes today.

COMPUTER Heroes!

Sergey Brin and Larry Page were young computer researchers when they created the PageRank algorithm in 1996. This algorithm ranked web pages in order of the number of **hyperlinks** they had to other web pages. This was the beginning of the Google search engine. Now the world's most popular search engine, Google's creators were ranked the 12th and 13th richest people in the world!

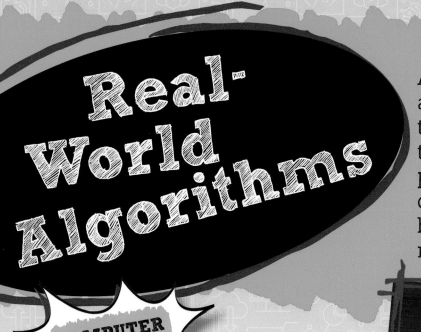

Web search engines use complex algorithms that search millions of websites for those web pages most relevant to the search words you type in.

 ## Pricing algorithms

Many algorithms are used to constantly check prices of items for sale on the World Wide Web. Companies use algorithms to search the websites of their competitors so they can match or beat their prices. The algorithms also gather information about demand for the item, and the range of prices it sells for. A price can be adjusted by the computer many times a day.

10

Shrinking sounds

Every time you listen to MP3 files of music or podcasts, you are hearing algorithms at work. MP3 is the name of an algorithm that reduces the size of a sound file by disregarding sounds in the file that you are unlikely to hear. This can help shrink the file to as little as a tenth of its original size. That means you can squeeze more tracks on to your smartphone, tablet, or music player.

Heating controls

Smart central-heating **controllers** make use of code containing algorithms to monitor and adjust room temperatures. Here is a simple algorithm that might be coded into a home heating controller:

1. Check what room temperature the user has set.
2. Measure actual temperature.
3. Display actual temperature on-screen.
4. If temperature is less than preferred temperature, turn on furnace.
5. If temperature is equal to or higher than preferred temperature, turn off furnace.

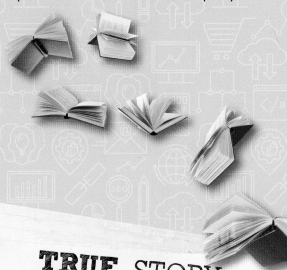

TRUE STORY

High-Flying Prices In 2011, two different booksellers using different pricing algorithms pushed the price of a book about flies sky-high! One algorithm upped the price of the book 27% higher than its competitor. The other algorithm changed the price to almost match the first. So each day the book's price rose until it reached over $23.6 million US on Amazon.com! Days later, the algorithms were corrected, and the book's price dropped to $106 US.

Sensors

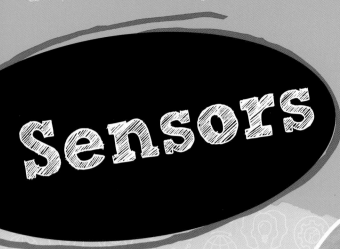

A sensor is a device that measures something in its surroundings. It is used in computer-controlled systems to provide vital information that the computer and its programs can act on.

Motion sensor

Security systems

Advanced security systems use many different types of sensors to keep a building or room secure. If any of these sensors are triggered, they send signals to the computer, which may decide to sound an alarm and alert law enforcement or security guards.

Some modern street lights feature sensors which measure how much light is reaching street level. The sensors send back data to the controller, which may adjust how intensely the street lights shine.

Tilt sensors: These measure the angle of an object. Attached to windows, they can detect if a window which should be closed has been opened.

Motion sensors: Some work by sending out thin beams of **infrared light**. If a beam is broken by someone moving through it, the sensor will send a signal to the security computer.

Pressure sensors: Placed under rugs or doormats, these can measure if something heavy steps on the mat, such as an intruder.

Control panel: A computer that controls the security system is contained in the control panel. Data from the sensors enters the control panel **wirelessly**.

Car computers

A modern car is packed full of sensors, which feed back information to the car's computer. Some sensors measure the condition of certain parts, such as the air pressure of the tires, or how the different parts of the brakes or engine are performing.

An oxygen sensor measures how much unburned fuel reaches the exhaust of a car. The sensor sends back measurements to the car's computer, which might adjust how much fuel it lets into the engine as a result.

Parking sensors

Many vehicles are equipped with sensors that use sound waves to detect distances when a car reverses or needs to park in a tight space. The sensor sends out ultrasonic sound waves, which are waves that are too high-pitched for people to hear. The waves bounce off nearby objects. The time it takes for the sound to return is converted by the car's computer into a measurement of how far away the object is.

The car's computer will display the distance on the driver's dashboard. It might also be programmed to warn the driver with a sound if the vehicle gets within a specified distance.

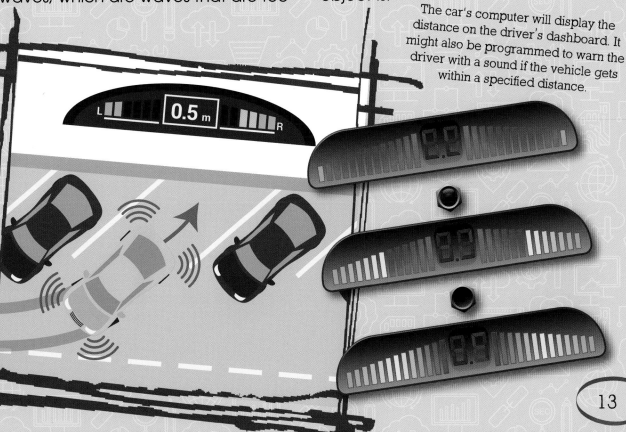

0.5 m

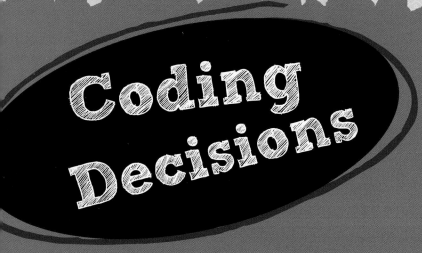

Coding Decisions

Many tasks in real-world computing require the program to make decisions. It might make these decisions after comparing different pieces of information or in response to input from a human user.

 ## IF—THEN statements

IF—THEN statements are often used in decision-making. This kind of statement says, "IF something is true or occurs, THEN the program will respond in a certain way." For example, to heat water to 212°F (100°C), a smart kettle might have this simple algorithm in its controller:

IF water temperature = 212°F (100°C), THEN turn off power

 ## IF—THEN—ELSE

You can add ELSE to an algorithm decision. This acts like the word "instead," and makes the program do something else if the IF statement is not true or does not occur. For example:

IF water temperature = 212°F (100°C), THEN switch off power, ELSE continue heating water.

Or for a quiz on a smartphone:

IF answer is correct, THEN add one to score and display "Well Done," ELSE display "Wrong!" and make a raspberry sound.

Programs hang onto key information in small storage areas called variables. Some computing decisions involve checking whether information entered by the user matches a variable stored in the program.

Here is a simple algorithm to check whether a user has typed in the correct password. In this example, the password stored in the program is a variable named Pword.

1. Ask the person to type in their password.
2. Make whatever is typed in become a variable called User.
3. IF User = Pword, THEN start program, ELSE display "Invalid Password" and return to 1.

The ELSE statement means, if the password typed in does not match the password held in the memory, the program will show "Invalid Password" and take the user back to the start to request the password again.

Flowcharting

A diagram called a **flowchart** is useful for mapping out where decisions and steps go in an algorithm. A flowchart consists of blocks in shapes that identify their purpose. The blocks are joined by arrows that create a path.

Terminators: The start or end of a program.

Input/Output: Input is data taken in from sensors or put in by a user. Output is the form in which the results are given to the user. Examples include a message on the screen or a warning sound.

Processes" Events where something happens, such as adding two numbers together.

Decisions: When a program makes a decision, such as yes or no. (The black flow lines show which step each decision takes you to.)

Decide to bake a cake

Ingredients list for cake

Mix ingredients

Bake in oven

Not Ready

Test with a fork

Ready

Remove from oven; let cool

Ice cake

Serve on plates

STRETCH YOURSELF

Decision Makers

Can you add a diamond shape to the flowchart (at right) to check and decide if the cake is cool enough to ice? Add flow lines to show where each decision takes you. (See answer on page 31.)

In Control

Unlike humans, computers never get tired of doing the same task over and over again. This makes them great at controlling events and processes that last all day, every day, such as running machines in factories or traffic lights.

 Green-fingered computing

Automated greenhouses check on plants and growing conditions minute by minute, without human supervision. The greenhouse contains large numbers of sensors which measure the amount of light reaching the plants, as well as the air temperature inside the greenhouse, and the amount of moisture in the soil. The sensors act as input devices, collecting data and sending it to the computer.

 Computer monitoring

Many computers work 24 hours a day checking other machines or systems. For example, in the picture above, this control panel in an oil refinery displays the computer's regular measurements of systems to ensure they run smoothly.

The computer monitors data in the greenhouse and controls output devices such as water pumps, lights that mimic sunlight, and heaters to control growing conditions inside.

Part of the algorithm for the greenhouse computer might be:

1. Receive input from heat sensor.
2. IF temperature too cold, THEN send signal to turn on greenhouse heater.
3. IF temperature too hot, THEN send signal to motors to open windows to let cooler air in.
4. Go back to 1 to repeat process.

CNC machining

First developed in the 1950s, Computer Numerical Control (CNC) computers instruct factory machine tools that cut, drill, and shape materials into parts to manufacture products. This is called machining. CNC computers contain programs with all the instructions required for the machine to produce the part accurately. CNC machines can run for long periods, producing parts accurately with little or no human supervision.

STRETCH YOURSELF

Parking Lot Barriers
Some parking lots have simple computer control with sensors alerting the computer to raise an arm barrier each time a car enters or leaves. Create a simple algorithm in written English to describe the process.

☞ Can your algorithm decide whether a car is entering or leaving?

☞ Can you add to your algorithm so that you can keep count of the number of cars in the parking lot?

Barcodes and Stock Control

Every time you buy something from a store, coding is at work behind the scenes. Items on sale are all identified with a universal product code, or UPC. These codes are usually displayed on the product as a series of lines known as a barcode.

 Scanning devices

A barcode scanner can be a handheld machine or be fitted into a glass-topped panel at checkouts. A scanner shines a light that bounces off the lines that make up a barcode. A sensor called a photocell collects the reflected light, and a decoder device inside the scanner converts the lines into a 12-digit UPC number. A beep usually sounds to indicate that the scan has been successful.

AC574D90A

An item is scanned at the checkout. The scanner converts the barcode's black and white lines into numbers. This is the product's stock number. The code number is sent to a central computer, which contains the **database** of all the stock the store sells.

A search through the database matches the barcode to the product and confirms its price. The database stock is updated at the time of sale to record one less item in stock.

The price is sent back to the checkout, where it is displayed on-screen. A running total of all items purchased is kept to produce the shopper's receipt, which is printed out.

18

What have we got?

Barcodes help stores know what they have sold and how many of each item they have left in stock. Barcodes are also used to track deliveries of goods and manage **inventory** in warehouses and factories. This allows companies to keep track of where items are and how many they have left. Many libraries also use scanning for checking books in and out.

STRETCH YOURSELF

Create a Code

If you or your family have a website, you can create your own QR code. When scanned by a tablet or smartphone, it will open your web page in the device's browser. To find out how, head to:

👉 www.qr-code-generator.com/

Type in your website or web page address and click on the "Create QR" code button. Your very own QR code will appear on the right for you to download.

QR CODES

Quick response (QR) codes are square codes that can hold much more information than a standard barcode. A QR code can be read using a camera on a smartphone, run by a free app. Some QR codes contain a website address as a hyperlink to a special offer or discount. Scanning the code calls up the web page in the phone's web browser.

COMPUTER Hero!

6 901234 567843

Two young men invented the barcode system before they had even used a computer. Americans Bernard Silver and Joseph Woodland came up with the idea in 1949, after drawing lines in the sand in Florida. However, the first product to use a barcode was not sold until 1974. It was a pack of chewing gum.

Where Am I?

Coding in many computers and other devices help with **navigation**. They help people locate where they are or how far they have traveled. Some are able to figure out the best route to reach a final destination.

Fitness trackers

Fitness trackers worn on the wrist measure the number of steps you take, using some clever computing. Sensors called accelerometers use the swing of your arm and the tilt of your body as you move, to measure the distance and direction you have traveled. The code in a fitness tracker ignores small movements and converts larger ones into the number of steps taken and the overall distance covered.

Global Positioning System

Satellites orbiting 12,550 miles (20,200 kilometers) above Earth provide 24-hour navigation on the planet's surface. Known as the **Global Positioning System (GPS)**, it works using microprocessors, which are complete computing units, each on a single tiny chip. The chips in GPS receivers are programmed to seek radio signals sent at the same time from a number of satellites.

GPS works by measuring the amount of time it takes for each satellite's signal to reach a receiver's device. The coding in the device converts the time into distance. By knowing the distance away from three or more satellites, the receiver's device can display its own location to within a few feet (meters).

GPS uses

GPS receivers are found in vehicles, boats, some smartphones, and in wearable GPS devices worn by hikers, skiers, and runners. Wildlife researchers fit miniature GPS devices to birds and animals to track their movements and to learn more about their travels and behavior.

Mapping a journey

Mapping programs use GPS to place a person or a vehicle's current position on maps stored in the memory. The position updates as the person or vehicle moves. Such programs also use algorithms to determine the shortest route, in either time or distance, from where the user is to their final destination.

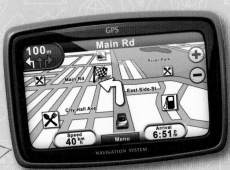

Shortest path

One method used by computers to calculate the shortest route is to split up all the potential routes into different points along the way. These are called **nodes**, shown as black circles in the diagram below. They are connected by links, shown on the diagram as lines. There might be hundreds or thousands of nodes on a route. Computer algorithms use different techniques to select which nodes and in what order the route should follow, based on time or distance.

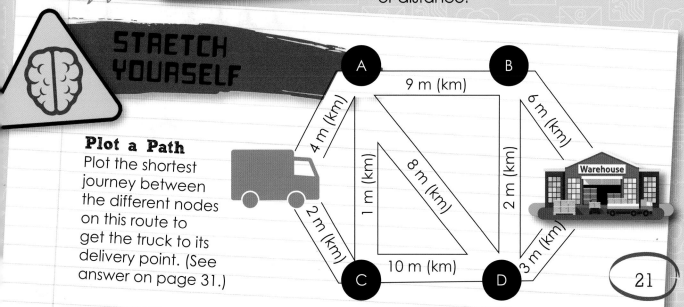

STRETCH YOURSELF

Plot a Path

Plot the shortest journey between the different nodes on this route to get the truck to its delivery point. (See answer on page 31.)

A — 9 m (km) — B

4 m (km)

6 m (km)

1 m (km)

8 m (km)

2 m (km)

2 m (km)

Warehouse

C — 10 m (km) — D

3 m (km)

Money Matters

Less than 15% of all money transactions in the world actually use coins and bills. Most transactions are in electronic form, constantly flowing between computers all around the world.

Cash dispenser

Every time someone visits an automated teller machine (ATM), or cash dispenser, they are converting some of the money in their bank account into cash. The bank card they put in the machine has a magnetic strip that contains the user's bank account details. When the card is inserted, the ATM is programmed to connect to the bank's computer network to send and receive data and instructions.

The card's strip is read by the magnetic reader inside the machine, which converts the data into signals.

The signals carrying the details of the card are sent to the bank computer.

Once the card is recognized, the screen displays a message asking for a code called a Personal Identificatiion Number (PIN). The user enters their PIN, which is also sent to the bank's, computer.

xxxx

If the user asks for a receipt, the ATM instructs its small printer to print one.

$ 25

Once the details are confirmed by the bank's computer, the user can request cash, which travels up from the ATM's mini vault on rollers.

The bank's computers contain a database of bank account information. The details on the card are compared to the bank's database. The computer is programmed to decline the transaction if, for example, the card has been reported stolen or if the user requests more money than they have in their account.

 ## Wide Area Network

A bank's network of ATMs and the computers inside its branches form what is called a wide area network (WAN). They are all connected to a central computer or set of computers, and must be coded accurately so all the machines can communicate with one another.

CONTACTLESS CARDS

New bank cards allow people to pay for goods just by placing their card close to a card reader. This is coded to send out radio signals over a short distance when a transaction is about to be made.

A loop of copper wire inside the contactless card acts as a radio antenna, picking up the signals.

A contactless card's microchip holds the user's account details, which are sent to the card reader.

The card reader is programmed to send the details to a computer, which confirms the bank details and makes the payment.

Working with Robots

Robots are programmable machines. Some can explore places humans cannot get to, perform work too precise or difficult for humans, or carry out repeated tasks without tiring.

Key parts

All robots have sensors that gather information about the robot or its surroundings. This data is sent to the robot's computer, known as a controller. The controller's code makes decisions based on the information from the sensors. It instructs other parts of the robot to move or work in some way.

Sensors in a robot vacuum cleaner alert its controller that an obstacle is in the way. The controller's program can then plot a new path around the room.

Control and code

Robots without their programs are far from smart! They require programming in order to function. Many robot controllers are reprogrammable, so that the entire robot can be instructed to perform different sets of tasks after new code is uploaded.

TRUE STORY

Rapid Robots! Some robots are amazingly fast and tireless performers. At a car manufacturer in China, for example, a team of robot arms can make all the 4,000 different welds required to build a Haval SUV vehicle body in just 86 seconds!

Robot anatomy

The majority of working robots are not human-like in shape. They vary in design, from crawling snakebots that can examine the inside of pipelines to powerful robot arms and rovers with wheels or tracks that explore deserts, hazardous areas, or even other planets.

COMPUTER Hero!

In 1961, George Devol and Joseph Engelberger developed and programmed the first robot that worked for a living. Unimate was a robot arm that handled red-hot metal in a factory making cars. It worked 100,000 hours before it was retired.

Remote control or autonomous?

Some robot-like devices, such as flying drones, are remote-controlled by a human operator who sends commands through a cable or radio signals. Other robots work without human control or supervision once programmed. These are known as autonomous robots.

STRETCH YOURSELF

Design a Robot

Grab some paper and pens and design two of the following three robots:

1. A robot that searches for survivors in fires and collapsed buildings,

2. A lawn-mowing robot,

3. A human-like robot that greets visitors and shows them around a museum.

Think about the following questions:

☞ What sort of hazards or obstacles would each robot face?

☞ What sort of sensors would each type of robot require?

☞ What sort of algorithms would each robot need to perform its task safely?

3-D Printing

A regular printer receives a digital file from a computer, and the program code helps turn it into a form that can be output onto paper. 3-D printers perform a similar job, but instead of a flat printout, they build 3-D objects, with height, length, and depth.

⬇ Layer by layer

3-D printers "print" by applying a thin layer of material, usually a type of plastic stored on spools, like wire. Each layer is often just 0.1 mm thick, so the printer has to print many layers to complete an object.

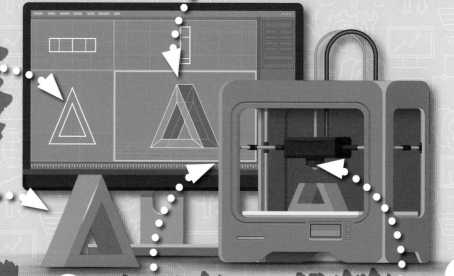

1
An accurate 3-D model is produced on a computer. It is usually created using a computer-aided design (**CAD**) program which allows people to design 3-D objects on-screen.

2
Sometimes, an additional program called a slicer is needed. This analyzes the object and produces code describing the object slice by thin slice. Hundreds or thousands of slices may make up an object.

5
The completed object is exactly the same shape as the digital model stored on the computer.

3
The final file is sent to the 3-D printer. The file contains code which instructs the printer about what it should print for each layer.

4
The 3-D printer's head passes over the object many times, building it up layer by layer. A large or complex object can take many hours of printing.

RAPID PROTOTYPING

3-D printers were invented in the 1980s, but it is only in the last ten years that their use has really taken off. One of their most important uses is called rapid prototyping. 3-D printing allows engineers and inventors to produce early, single versions of their products, called prototypes, quickly and easily, without having to take it to a factory.

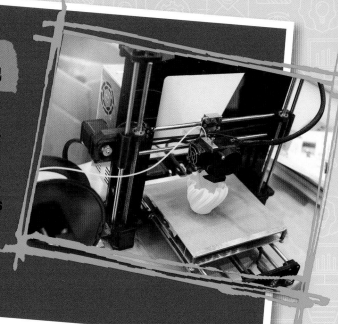

 ## 3-D industry

3-D printing is already a big industry, producing everything from personalized toys and souvenirs to human body parts, such as false teeth and artificial hands.

3-D printing is increasingly used for creating parts for vehicles and other machines. The new Airbus A350 WXB airliner, for example, contains more than 1,000 parts printed in 3-D.

A 3-D printer produces a model of a human spine.

TRUE STORY

Print Your Own Car American car company Local Motors produced an electric car whose entire body was printed out of plastic strengthened with carbon fibers. The Strati took 44 hours to print on a giant 3-D printer. It could travel over 110 miles (180 km) before having to recharge its batteries.

The Internet of Things

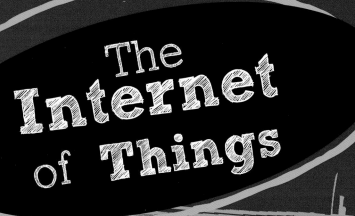

As more and more devices are made containing computer technology, coding is developed to connect them. Many devices link through the Internet. They can be programmed to share information, and be controlled by other devices or by human users. All these connected devices are known together as the Internet of Things.

Intelligent appliances

All sorts of household appliances can be coded to communicate with other devices, often wirelessly. Some washing machines, for example, link to the owner's smartphone to send them a message that the wash cycle is completed. New Internet-enabled fridges use cameras to keep track of objects stored inside. They can add items to an electronic shopping list as well as alert the owner when food is past its expiry date!

Connected highways

Roads that have signs and sensors connected to the Internet can share information with vehicles while managing the traffic flow. Vehicles can be quickly alerted to roadwork or accidents ahead. Traffic signals can be altered to help emergency vehicles reach their destination rapidly.

Street smart

Many devices are being coded to connect to the Internet to exchange information in useful ways. Streetlights, for example, can send back data to a repair center when they need to be fixed or have bulbs replaced. Smart garbage cans can alert waste collectors when they need emptying.

SMART HOMES

Linked together, a number of devices can form a smart home. Lights, heating, cooling, and many other features can be controlled by a single program running on a tablet or other digital device.

Sensors can detect when everyone has gone to bed and turn off all spare lighting to save energy.

Smart ovens can be instructed by a smart fridge to turn on and warm up.

Security systems can send outside views of the home to the TV or tablet, or instruct all lights to come on.

A digital assistant can recognize a person's voice and send them reminders and to-do lists.

Users can control their TV and record programs through their tablet or smartphone.

Missing keys that are tagged with radio transmitters can be located using the control tablet.

Music or radio can be programmed to come on in different rooms at different times.

Glossary

3-D Describing an object that has, or appears to have, three dimensions: length (width), depth, and height

algorithm A set of steps that are followed in a certain order to solve a problem or perform a task

apps Short for applications, these are software programs downloaded and run on a smartphone or tablet

automated Acting without any outside instruction

Bluetooth A technology that allows computers and other devices to communicate with each other using radio signals instead of cables

CAD Short for computer-aided design, these are programs used to create complete models, often of buildings, structures, and mechanical parts

central processing unit (CPU) A microprocessor, or computing unit, that can perform millions of operations every second

code The line of instructions in a program that make a computer or other device work

controller The part of a computer that receives information from sensors and instructs the other parts of the device

data Pieces of information a user puts into a computer

database A type of computer program that allows people to store large amounts of information and perform searches and matches, and retrieve information easily

feedback Information obtained from the output of a computer that influences the input stage

flowchart A type of diagram that maps out the actions and decisions that occur within a computer program

Global Positioning System (GPS) A navigation system using satellites orbiting Earth to provide precise locations

hyperlink A word, phrase, or image on a web page, which, when clicked on, allows the user to jump to a new web page or a different website

infrared light A type of light we cannot see with our eyes but can feel as heat

input Adding data or a command into a program or computer system

inventory A complete list of items, such as goods in stock or the contents of a building

navigation The act of going from one place to another

network Two or more computers or digital devices linked together so they can communicate with one another

node A point on a plotted route, linked with lines

output The results of a computer's work on data that has been input

satellite A machine traveling in space around Earth that performs useful work, such as sending TV or Internet signals to different parts of the planet

sensor A device that detects or measures something such as sound or temperature in its environment, and sends back data to a computer

smart Any device that has the abiltiy to connect to the Internet built in

wirelessly Sent through technology that connects computers and other digital devices to each other and the Internet without wires or cables

World Wide Web A collection of information that can be accessed by the Internet

Further Resources

Books

I'm an App Developer (Generation Code)
by Max Wainewright (Crabtree Publishing, 2018)

Maker Projects for Kids Who Love Robotics by James Bow
(Crabtree Publishing, 2016)

Robotics (Crabtree Chrome) by Lynn Peppas
(Crabtree Publishing , 2015)

Websites

www.tynker.com/hour-ofcode/
*Learn in a fun and interactive way how coding works. The
Tynker programming area contains several simple games.*

www.whatisaqrcode.co.uk/
Learn more about QR codes and what they can do.

www.bbc.co.uk/schools/gcsebitesize/design/
systemscontrol/workingwithsystemsrev4.shtml
*See the algorithm and decision-making required for a
parking lot barrier to operate.*

https://code.org/curriculum/unplugged
*Check out this fun and informative collection of activities
to learn more about programming.*

Answers

page 15

Add this instruction to test
whether the cake is cool enough to ice.

```
        ┌──────────────────┐
        │  Remove from     │
        │  oven; let cool  │
        └──────────────────┘
                 │
  Not            ▼
  cool   ┌──────────────┐
         │  Test if cake│
         │  is cool to  │──── Cool
         │  the touch   │
         └──────────────┘
                 │
                 ▼
         ┌──────────────┐
         │   Ice cake   │
         └──────────────┘
```

page 21

Plot a Path Truck –> C > A > D >
Destination = 14 miles (14 km)

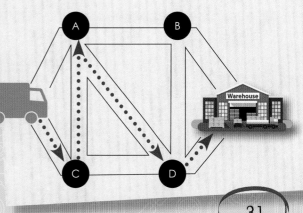

Index